RENO 2

RENO 2

The National Championship Air Races

MIKE JERRAM

Published in 1986 by Osprey Publishing Limited
27A Floral Street, London WC2E 9DP
Member company of the George Philip Group

British Library Cataloguing in Publication Data

Jerram, Michael F.
    Reno 2: the national championship air races.—
    Osprey colour series)
    1. Reno Air Races
    I. Title
    629.13′074′019355   GV759

ISBN 0-85045-702-5

Editor Dennis Baldry
Designed by David Tarbutt
Printed in Hong Kong

Front cover Racers come, racers go, but Bob
Hoover's *Yellowbird* P-51D is an institution at
Reno. Hoover acts as pace pilot and 'guardian
angel' for the Unlimited racers, and rarely resists
the opportunity to take a turn around the course
once his charges have safely landed

Title pages Steve Hinton's *Super Corsair* (left of
picture) shares the course with an AD-4N
Skyraider

Back cover Colour me quick. Lloyd Hamilton's
team could wear anything they liked so long as it
was red, to match the sanguine shade of *Furias'*
flanks

Mike Jerram is a freelance aviation writer and photographer. He is contributing editor of the British general aviation magazine *Pilot*, editorial consultant to the General Aviation Manufacturers & Traders Association, and part of the editorial team of *Jane's All The World's Aircraft*. His first book in the Osprey Colour Series, *War Birds*, was published in 1984. The photographs in this book were all taken with Nikon cameras and lenses, loaded with Kodachrome 25 and 64.

To my son, Robert.

With grateful thanks to Bill, Denis, Ken, Norm and Rick.

Contents

Power curves

Radial chic. The Sanders Racing Team line up at Reno included standard 'cooking' Sea Furies with the original sleeve valve Bristol Centaurus engine (Dale Clark's *Nuthin Special* in foreground) and the Pratt & Whitney R-4360 powered Super Sea Fury *Dreadnought*

Pages 10–14 Lloyd Hamilton's Santa Rosa, California-based racing team fielded another R-4360 Sea Fury, *Furias*, which made its Reno debut as *Head Gorilla* in 1983, and failed to reach the finals in 1984 after losing most of its cowling during a heat race. The 28-cylinder, four row R-4360 engine, popularly known as the 'corncob', puts out some 3800 hp, against the Bristol Centaurus' 2480 hp, and unlike the $50,000 race-prepared Rolls-Royce Merlins demanded by the P-51 racers the old corncobs can be had for $4000 or so. *Furias'* big banger, turning a Skyraider propeller, took Hamilton to 411.952 mph and fourth place in the Unlimited Gold race

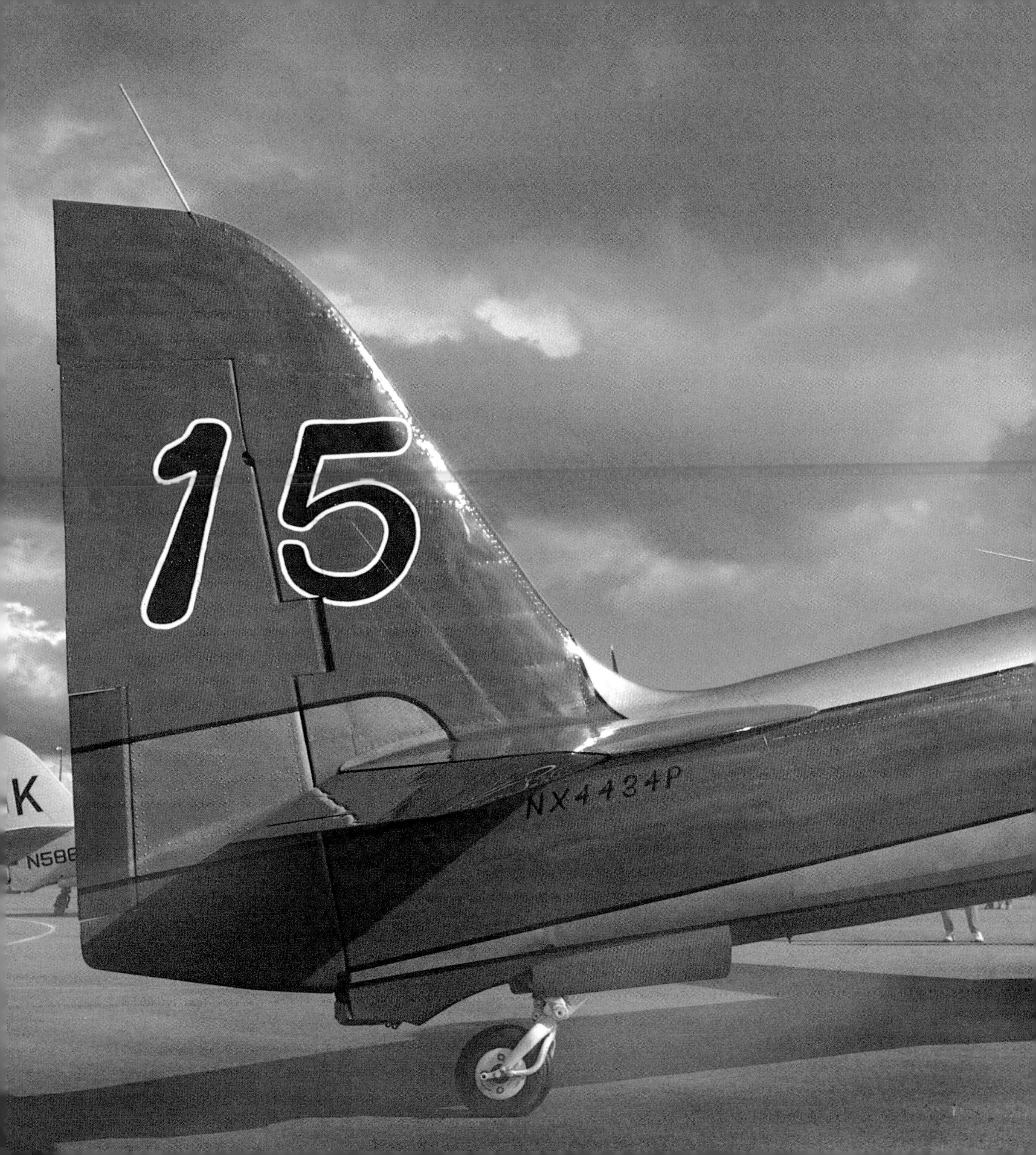

15
NX4434P
K
N586

There's no restriction on parking space on the Reno ramp, but Flying Tigers captain Richard Drury still chooses to fold away the wings of his #43 Sea Fury, which wears authentic early post-war Fleet Air Arm colours. Clark, making his Reno debut, gained sixth spot in the Silver division at 356.736 mph

Overleaf Frank Sanders' R-4360 Super Sea Fury *Dreadnought* was originally a Sea Fury T.20 delivered to Burma, from where it was recovered in 1979. *Dreadnought* won the Unlimited Championship on its first outing in 1983 at 425.242 mph in the hands of General Dynamics chief test pilot Neil Anderson. Apart from the corncob R-4360-63A engine grafted onto its nose

and a 13 ft 6 in Aeroproducts four-blade propeller, *Dreadnought* has an extended vertical fin and rudder for increased directional stability and a meticulously cleaned up airframe. 115/145 octane racing brew goes into port wing and fuselage tanks. The starboard wing tank holds water alcohol ADI fluid. Frank's Air Racing Team (colloquially known by the unflattering acronym FART) claim a maximum level speed in excess of 490 mph for Dreadnought

Waiting in the (gull) wings. Planes of Fame
Museum's clip-wing, R-4360 engined *Super
Corsair* lacked its former billboard sponsorship
logos at Reno 1985, but seems certain to be more
extensively decorated in 86 after Steve Hinton's
championship victory

Santa Monica attorney Bob Guildford is a veteran
campaigner in his stock F4U-7 Corsair #93 *Blue
Max* seen here taxying in after finishing ninth
(and last) in the Unlimited Bronze event. Speed:
282.904 mph

Bob Yancey's F4U-4 Corsair #101 *Old Blue* prepares for Unlimited Heat 1-B, which turned into a six lap long duel between Yancey and Dennis Sanders in Sea Fury #924, and provided some of the most exciting racing of the event

Right 'We came here to beat a Bearcat,' said Bob Yancey, and promptly ate up the entire field in Heat 1-B, coming from last to win over Dennis Sanders' Sea Fury by two tenths of a second. His pit crew quickly applied Sea Fury and Bearcat kill markings to *Old Blue*'s flanks

Dallas real estate developer Alan Preston brought his 1984 championship winning Mustang *Stiletto*, a Harvard and his F4U-5NL Corsair #12 *Old Deadeye* to Reno. The Corsair, a former night fighter variant racing minus the starboard wing radar pod which it wore in US Navy service, was flown by its former owner Bruce Lockwood. Going into the chute for the start of the first Unlimited Heat of the 1985 National Championship Air Races, *Old Deadeye*'s canopy suddenly exploded. 'It sounded like a quarter stick of dynamite going off. I don't know if I hit a bird or what,' declared a super cool Lockwood after a hurried landing. A substitute canopy and some patching of the fin and stabilizer got *Old Deadeye* into racing trim again by Sunday, when it placed sixth in the Bronze division

Preceding pages and above 1982 champion
Dago Red was back at Reno recovered from the
fire which forced it out of the Unlimited Gold
event in 84. Few Unlimited owners talk money,
but *Dago*'s master Frank Taylor allows that the
P-51's development left little change out of half a
million dollars

Right Lusting for victory, or gasping for air?

Owner Frank Taylor flew *Dago Red* to an FAI
Class C, Group 1 World Speed Record on 30 July
1983, covering a 15/25 kilometre course at
Mojave, California at 517.06 mph. **Right** Any
colour you like so long as it's red. *Dago Red*'s
pilot Rick Brickert explains his tactics after
clocking 412.122 mph in Unlimited Heat 3-A.
Brickert placed third in the Gold final, completing
the eight lap race at an average 426.848 mph.
Overleaf *Dago Red* with the wraps off

This page and overleaf No newcomer to Reno, *Georgia Mae* was formerly the late Jack Sliker's *Escape I*. The polished aluminium finish almost hurt your eyes in the clear Nevada air, and if it looks familiar, it should: owner Wiley Sanders, who runs a trucking company in Troy, Alabama, also owned the look-alike *Jeannie* which had a similar mirror-bright finish. John Putman flew *Georgia Mae*, qualifying at 418 mph and recording 387 mph in Thursday and Friday's heats, but on Saturday, after leading throughout Heat 3-B, Putman pulled off the power to save *Georgia*'s engine and let Lefty Gardner's P-51D *Thunderbird* slide through to win. In the subsequent landing *Georgia Mae* groundlooped in a gusting crosswind and was greviously damaged

World Airlines check captain John Crocker was a target for the Reno gremlins. With his slick Mustang *#6 Sumthin' Else* running well up with the leaders in Saturday's Heat 3-A, the P-51D's Merlin backfired, causing serious damage and threatening Crocker's place in the Gold final. Some midnight oil burning saw *Sumthin' Else* back on the start line come Sunday, only to pull out on lap five with a blown engine

Fly the flag. The former Howie Keefe P-51D *Miss America* is now owned by Washington businessman Ron Smyth who is blind, and has never seen his beautiful 'flying Old Glory'. Flown by ex-Royal Canadian Air Force pilot Bud Granley, a hard charger who left roostertails of desert dust with *Miss America*'s clipped wingtips, the Mustang reached the Gold final after a 420.287 mph win in Heat 2-B, but was forced to retire after five laps of the Championship race

Overleaf *Strega*, like *Dago Red*, is from the Bill 'Tiger' Destefani stable, and was on its third Reno outing in 1985. A cracked blower during the warm up for the start of Heat 2-A brought pilot Ron

Hevle back to the runway and meant a long night for *Strega*'s pit crew. Next day a carburettor problem again prematurely aborted Hevle's heat race on lap six. The run of misfortune continued into the Gold final, when a film of oil on the windscreen signalled a broken piston and Hevle dropped back from the pre-race formation before it climbed over the mountains for the run-in to the start. 'If I would have gotten over the rocks when the engine quit I would have had to bail out,' said a bitterly disappointed Hevle, whose pit crew had worked exhaustingly on *Strega* throughout the Championships

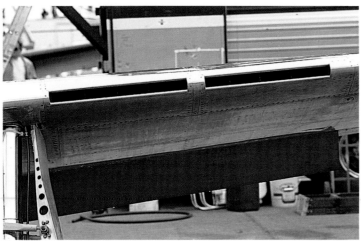

Alan Preston's #84 *Stiletto*, which won the 1984 Unlimited Championship at 437.62 mph, is thus far the most-modified P-51D to race at Reno. The characteristic ventral cooling scoop has been deleted and replaced by flush inlets in the wing leading edges and computer controlled cooling spraybars. *Stiletto*'s wing area has been savagely reduced to slightly less than that of a 100 hp Cessna 150 trainer. Pilot Skip Holm, an Edwards AFB trained test pilot, believes *Stiletto*, or something like it, can raise Reno race speeds to 490 mph. Engine and mechanical problems dogged his 1985 challenge, and a balky landing gear leg finally destroyed *Stiletto*'s chances of pulling off two consecutive wins

Formerly the all-conquering *Jeannie*, Jimmy Leeward's *Leeward Air Ranch Special* came to Reno high on the list of favourites for the Unlimited Gold, but was dogged with problems and failed to reach the final race

This page and overleaf Former cropduster and one of the founders of the Confederate Air Force, Lefty Gardner is a Reno regular in his P-38 Lightning #13 *White Lit'nin*, which he races and flies in the daily airshows. His racing is characterized by his ability to get the Lightning's wingtip closer to the desert than anyone else dares, while his aerobatic routine includes some spectacular engine-out work including low-level rolls into the dead engine—a technique once thought to be a certain way to 'buy the farm'. Lefty's P-38 is the only Unlimited racer at Reno which *intentionally* streams smoke from its engines: he has an effective smoke generating system with which he traces his aerobatic figures

Preceding pages, above and right Lyle
Shelton's modified F8F-2 Bearcat #77 *Rare Bear*
won at Reno in 1973 as the $7\frac{1}{4}\%$ *Special*, and
again in 1975 as the *Aircraft Cylinder Special*.
Huge ex-Skyraider propeller demands near three-
point take-offs and landings. At the 1985 races
Rare Bear was flown by local Sparks, Nevada,
man and former Lear Fan test pilot John Penney,
making his debut in the event. Penney's race
speed in Thursday's Heat 1-A was 407.502 mph,
putting the Bearcat among the fancied contenders
for Gold. Alas. . .

Dirty bear. During the Friday Gold division heat John Penney called a *Mayday* and pulled up streaming white vapour. A missing safety wire on an oil plug had allowed the *Rare Bear*'s life blood to be pumped overboard. After pulling off an exceptionally skilful deadstick landing in an aeroplane with the gliding characteristics of a concrete slab, Penney slithered off *Rare Bear*'s oil-washed wing roots to discover the engine totally seized

Clean bear. Howard Pardue's rare short fin F8F-1 Bearcat #14 waxed its way into fifth place in the Unlimited Silver division with a race speed of 359.415 mph

Action Unlimited

'Gentleman, you have a race!' Unseen in this picture, pace pilot Bob Hoover was already pulling up to maintain station above the course after releasing the Unlimited Gold contenders into the chute for the start of Friday's Heat 2-A. Steve Hinton in #1 *Super Corsair* and Neil Anderson flying #8 *Dreadnought* run neck and neck, with Skip Holm going low in #84 *Stiletto* while Rick Brickert in #4 *Dago Red*, John Crocker in #6 *Sumthin' Else* and John Penney aboard #77 *Rare Bear* go high into the first turn. Anderson took the heat at 424. 796 mph, closely followed by Hinton

Overleaf Aural ecstacy for Unlimited fans as ten thousand or more horses combine to limber up in the ramp area before the start of Heat 2-B

This page and overleaf Boat manufacturer Dale Clark from Covina, California, got down among the sagebrush in his two-seat Sea Fury #40 *Nuthin Special*, battling hard with Howard Pardue's F8F-1 Bearcat in Unlimited Heat 3-C. The Bearcat finally got the better of him, taking first at 356.087 mph. The close companionship continued in the Silver fly-off, with Clark finishing just three miles per hour behind fifth place Pardue

Left 63 year-old veteran Lefty Gardner had two cracks at the Unlimited races with his P-38 *White Lit'nin* and P-51D *Thunderbird*, the latter seen here rounding pylon 6 during Saturday's Heat 3-B which Lefty won at 377.321 mph. The USAF Thunderbirds never actually flew P-51Ds, but who would argue with such a gorgeous colour scheme?

Lefty Gardner's P-38 #13 *White Lit'nin* is part racer, part airshow mount. Though uncompetitive with the best Unlimiteds, the fork-tailed devil gets lower than anything else as Lefty dusts the desert, and gained a creditable fourth in the Bronze division. Hung-up nosewheel door, just visible in this picture, must have imposed a drag penalty

Flying Tiger Line captain Richard Drury made his Reno debut in Sea Fury #43, and took second in the Bronze division at 345.903 mph

Right Sunlight makes a chequerboard pattern of unpainted metals on Dale Clark's Sea Fury #40 *Nuthin Special* as he pulls around pylon 2

Left Jimmie McMillan's Douglas AD-4N Skyraider really did lead Skip Holm's slippery *Stiletto*, but only for this brief moment during the Unlimited qualifying runs. The lumbering Spad did make it through to the finish of racing, though, gaining seventh place in the Bronze division

Bob Yancey's Thursday battle with Dennis Sanders during Unlimited Heat 1-B was a high spot of the races. Yancey took his F4U-4 Corsair *Old Blue* from last place to beat Sanders' Sea Fury #924 by just .22 of a second. 'It was kinda exciting,' he allowed modestly. *Old Blue* took second place in Sunday's Silver final, clocking 374.392 mph

His race number may have been zilch, but 24 year-old John Maloney took fourth place in the Unlimited Silver event in his Chino, California based P-51D *Spam Can*

Left Crinkle-cut bear. Late afternoon sun catches every corrugation in the skin of Howard Pardue's F8F-1 Bearcat #14. Pardue, an oil and gas producer from Breckenridge, Texas, flies about 600 hours each year, all of them in warbirds

Overleaf Tom Kelley's P-51D *Lou IV* suffered a pressure instrument failure during the Unlimited Heat 3-B on Saturday. With no airspeed, vertical speed or altitude information, Kelley formated with safety pilot Bob Hoover down to the runway at Stead Airport, but was flying again on Sunday to take the Silver race at 374.418 mph

Left Bill 'Tiger' Destefani's much modified P-51D *Strega*, flown by 1982 champion Ron Hevle, was much fancied as a possible Unlimited winner but suffered engine problems and finally withdrew from the Gold event before the start with a broken piston

Above Formerly *Jeannie*, Jimmy Leeward's *Leeward Air Ranch Special* has the longest pedigree of all the Unlimiteds, having competed in the post-war Thompson Trophy events as a stock P-51D named *The Galloping Ghost*. Trouble-plagued throughout the week, Leeward finally pulled out with a broken cylinder during Saturday's Heat 3-B. 'Maybe next year,' he consoled himself

Overleaf A gusting crosswind caught Wiley Sanders' P-51D *Georgia Mae* on landing after finishing second in Heat 3-B, and the beautifully prepared Mustang went off into the sagebrush. Pilot John Putman was unhurt; *Georgia Mae* was severely damaged, but owner Sanders immediately declared her rebuildable

Above Last of the hard luck stories. Alan Preston's #84 *Stiletto* was favoured to achieve its second consecutive Reno victory. Despite a thrown rod and an engine change during qualification, the heavily modified Mustang was on the start line for Sunday's Gold final, but after take-off the right gear leg refused to retract and although pilot Skip Holm's indulged in some aerobatic, G-pulling efforts to stow the gear, he was unable to get *Stiletto* cleaned-up in time for the airborne start and had to retire

Preceding pages Rick Brickert brings Frank Taylor's P-51D *Dago Red* home after running fourth in Heat 2-A. *Dago*, given its head, added nearly 40 mph to its heat speed in the Gold final, placing third at 426.848 mph

Streaming vapour from underwing radiator spraybars, the Sanders Super Sea Fury *Dreadnought* lived up to its name, consistently leading the Unlimited field throughout the heat races, with a fastest speed of 436.947 mph on Saturday. Next day pilot Neil Anderson again led the pack from the outset, harried but never quite caught by Steve Hinton in *Super Corsair*.

Incredibly, rounding the final pylon on the last lap of the Gold final, Anderson cut inside the turn. Though he took the chequered flag, race officials penalized him 16 seconds for the cut giving the Championship to Hinton, who was just four seconds behind. 'I was watching a temperature gauge and suddenly the pylon wasn't there,' admitted F-16 test pilot Anderson. 'You just get too busy'

Left and overleaf Hail to the champion. After several years as bridesmaid, the Planes of Fame Museum's Chino-based *Super Corsair* finally took first spot at Reno, albeit thanks to Neil Anderson's only slip of the four days of racing. *Super Corsair* is powered by a 4360 cubic inch, 26 cylinder, four row Pratt & Whitney R-4360 radial engine driving a Douglas Skyraider propeller. Power output is around 3800 hp. Fuel consumption? If you have to ask you can't afford it, but figure on 400 US gallons per hour at race speeds. Steve Hinton clocked 438.186 mph for the Gold final, setting a new Reno race record and giving the Corona, California-based pilot his first Reno victory since 1978, when he took the Unlimited Championship in the RB-51 *Red Baron* and nearly died a year later in the desert crash which followed an engine seizure and totally demolished the much-modified, Griffon-engined Mustang

AT-6/SNJ class

Left San Joaquin, California, ag pilot Jerry McDonald bought his SNJ-4 *Big Red* 'on a whim' in 1978. He took the AT-6 class Silver race at Reno 85, narrowly beating Alan Preston in old campaigner #44, *Miss Behavin'*. McDonald's race speed was 216.236 mph

Above Jimmy Gist's signwriter had another line to add to *Texas Red*'s tally shortly after this picture was taken: 1985 4th Gold Div. 209.071 mph

Overleaf Down the chute. Charlie Beck's SNJ-4 *Honest Entry* leads *Warlock*, *Silver Baby* and *Rent-A-Dent* to the start line for Heat 1-C on the first day of racing

Bill and Bud Arnot had a matched pair of racers at Reno. T-6 *Silver Baby* took sixth place in the Silver Division flown by Charles Hutchins of Texas City. Their B-25J Mitchell *Silver Lady* cruised around the course but failed to qualify

Always among the best prepared and glossiest AT-6/SNJs is Al Goss' SNJ-6 *Warlock*, 'Quick Son of a Witch', which was runner-up in the Gold final at 213.682 mph

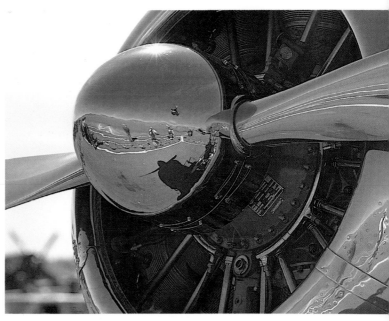

Above No engine or airframe modifications are permitted in the AT-6/SNJ class, but you may wax and polish to your heart's content (or until you arms ache, which they surely will). Bakersfield, California, refuse contractor John Martin's SNJ-5 *Boog* gets the elbow grease treatment, which helped it to Bronze second place at 200.725 mph

Left and right Charlie Beck, a building contractor from Olivenhain, California, really had his nose rubbed in it. The 62 year-old veteran combat pilot who flew 68 World War 2 missions in P-47s and P-51s, pulled out of Heat 1-C on Thursday with a suspected loose propeller blade. Proving the old adage that a T-6 is never safely landed until it is tied down, he put *Honest Entry* onto its nose while attempting to correct an incipient groundloop. Beck was unhurt and with new propeller, cowl, and help from fellow T-6 racers, *Honest Entry* was back in the air two days later

Left and top Sinister black SNJ-5 *Mis-Chief* was raced by Jim Mott, who motored around the Reno sagebrush at indecently low-level but was penalized for five plyon cuts and relegated to sixth and last place in the AT-6/SNJ Gold final

Above Eddie Van Fossen's SNJ-4 *Miss TNT* exploded into fifth place in the Gold final

From Casper, Wyoming came The Tired Iron Racing Team's SNJ-5 *Wildcatter*, winner of the Bronze division at 202.528 mph. Pilot Mike Wright had a backseat passenger aboard only for his pre-race qualification runs

Left Cockpit canopies no lower than the oil can marker on the pylon is the byword at Reno. Jim Fox bends *Terrible Texan* around a midfield turn-point during the AT-6/SNJ Bronze race

T-6ers just love to fly, and free of the need to conserve temperamental, race-tuned engines, spend more time in the air practising at Reno than any of the other classes. This unmarked example didn't race, but cruised the course during qualification days. And why not?

Overleaf First time Reno racer Randy Difani heading for the finish line in the AT-6/SNJ Gold final in #18 *Thunderbolt*, ahead of #75 *Warlock*, #73 *Miss Everything*, #68 *Texas Red* and #27 *Miss TNT*. Difani, who works on 'classified projects' with Northrop Corporation, painted his AT-6A in the colours of the 56th Fighter Group's P-47s and led the final from the start. Race speed: 213.892 mph

Below Lust in the dust: artwork on Robert Heale's SNJ-5 *Lickety Split*

Right Charlie Beck's *Honest Entry* acquired a prop tip and cowling 'kill' marking in addition to this pylon-hugging logo after it nosed over

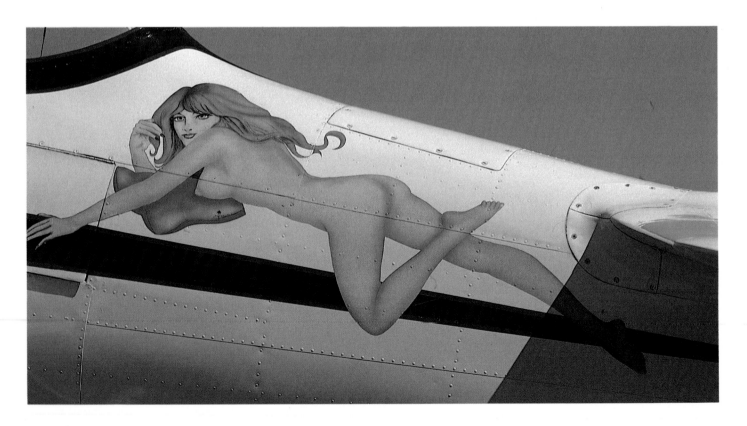

Formula 1 and Racing Biplanes

1982 F1 champion John Sharp was a strong favourite for the title again in 1985, but a balky engine prevented him starting in Heat 2-A, and he momentarily took the wrong course in Heat 1-A, losing his lead and a place in the Gold final.
Left *AeroMagic* rounds pylon Inner 6 during the Bronze event, which Sharp won at 230.513 mph—faster than Gold champion Ray Cote's race speed

Heading for Silver. Airline pilot Errol Johnstad came from West Berlin, Germany, to race his Cassutt 3M *Spring Fever*, and was rewarded with victory in the Silver event, postponed by strong winds until the last day of the races. Johnstad clocked 210.096 mph and attributed his victory to 'not doing anything stupid', though second placer Lori Love declared she would have 'had him if there had been one more lap'

Heading for home. Gary Hubler's Cassutt *Black Magic* failed to start in the Bronze race and was promptly loaded onto its trailer for the road journey back to Caldwell, Idaho

Not so wise. Portland, Oregon car wash equipment distributor Kirk Hanna qualified his Owl Racer *Wise Owl* at 224.386 mph in the Gold group, but was disqualified from the final for low flying

Overleaf Former astronaut Deke Slayton, flying #21 *Stinger*, fought a close run battle throughout the races with Lori Love, the only woman contestant at Reno 85. Slayton and Love swapped second and third places through the heat races, but Love finally pipped Slayton in the Silver event, taking second place while *Stinger* ran third at 208.725 mph

Preceding pages For the eleventh time veteran racer Ray Cote took the Formula 1 Gold title at Reno flying his Wagner Special #44 *Judy*. 'It makes me feel good to win,' declared Cote superfluously, 'but I have some empathy for the losers, because I've been there too.' *Judy's* race speed in the Gold final was 229.092 mph, though Cote's record for the F1 course at Reno stands unbeaten at 246.06 mph in his famous racer *Shoestring*. With eleven victories under his belt, Cote said he was thinking of selling *Judy* and becoming a spectator at Reno 86 . . . but don't bet on it

Above Construction engineer Dennis Brown had a video camera mounted on the centre section handgrip of Pitts #29 *Scarlet*, and filmed himself en route to third place in the Biplane Silver event

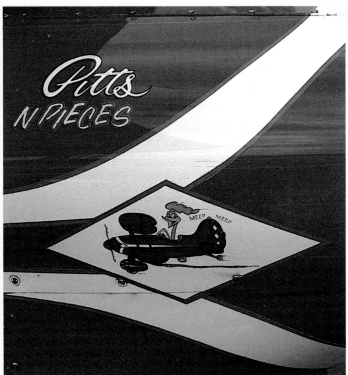

Very punny. Earl Allen's *Pitts-n-Pieces* was the fastest of the Pitts Specials in the Biplane Class. Pilot Del Schulte took it to 144.703 mph and fifth place in the Gold division

The two Dons, Fairbanks and Beck, are old campaigners in the Biplane class with Knight Twister Imperial #5 *White Knight* (preceding pages) and the much modified Smith Miniplane #00 *Miss Lake Tahoe* (this spread) respectively. In 1985, 61 year-old Fairbanks, who set a Sport Biplane class qualifying record at Reno a year earlier, was just 0.9 mph behind 63 year-old Beck in Heat 1-A, but in Sunday's Gold final *Miss Lake Tahoe* took the flag at 195.623 mph, while *White Knight* ran second at 177.665 mph. 'Dedication and concentration are the keys to winning,' said five times Biplane champ Beck

Reno reflections

Left *Super Corsair* basks in glory and late afternoon sunlight in front of the Reno grandstands after taking the 1985 Unlimited championship

This page and overleaf Its jubilant crew pop some cold ones even before Unlimited Champion Steve Hinton is out of *Super Corsair's* cockpit. Hinton still wasn't sure that he'd won as he taxied up to crowd centre, but was soon in little doubt. 'It's always good to be the underdog,' he said. And even better to be the winner

Above and right Hinton speaks to the media

Bud Granley briefly spurned the charms of *Miss America* to explain Unlimited air racing to the girls from Reno's Peppermill Casino

Right and overleaf The Casper, Wyoming-based Tired Iron Racing Team brought their B-26C Invader *Puss & Boots* to Reno, and unexpectedly gained a starting position in the Unlimited Bronze race. Mike Wright cruised the big bomber to sixth place at 283.96 mph

Bottom right Some chicken, some neck. Howard Pardue had a neat line in pitot head covers for his F8F-1 Bearcat

Below A pylon judge's badge is a much sought after item at Reno. The judges, all unpaid volunteers, watch for infringements and pylon cuts throughout the qualification runs, heats and final races

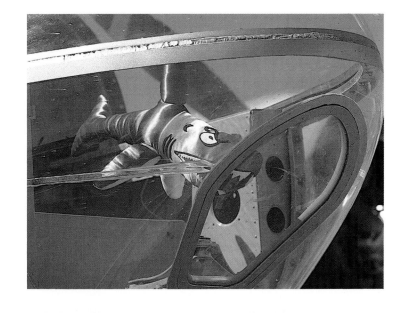

Forty-eight hours after these pictures were taken the legendary 'Professor' Art Scholl was dead, lost in the crash of a Pitts Special during a movie filming scqucncc off thc California coast. Scholl, who had a PhD in Aeronautics, delighted Reno crowds with his spectacular, pyrotechnic Super Chipmunk routine, and his crazy flying in a Super Cub in Saturday's gusts, hovering on the breeze and making unbelievable flat turns in front of the grandstands. His dog *Aileron* was a constant companion, occasionally accompanying Scholl in his Chipmunk displays

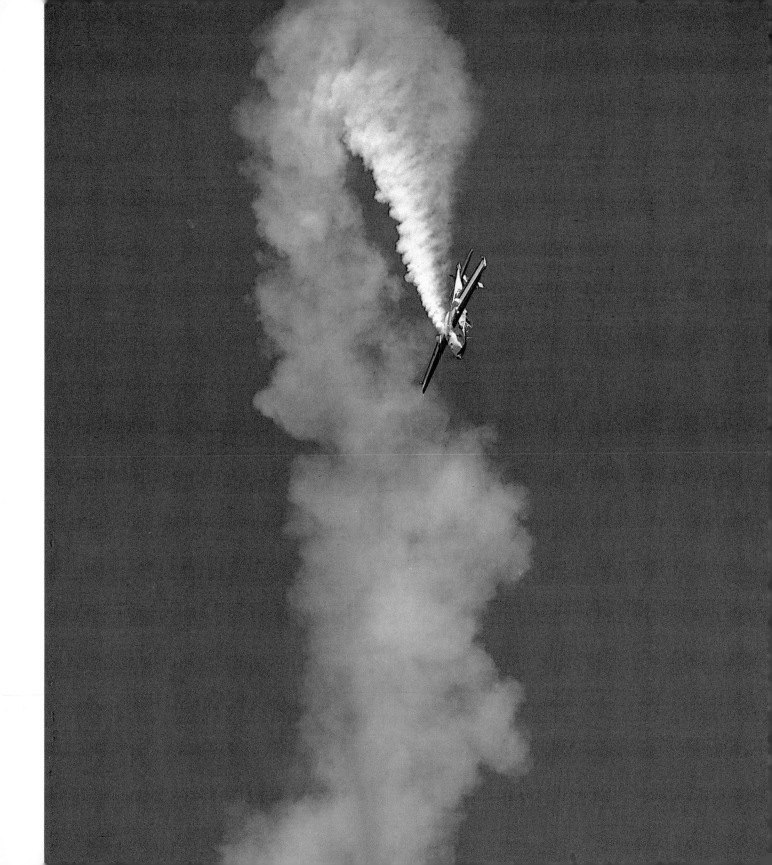